PATCHWORK MEMORIES

Cheryl,
Happy Quilting!
Retta Warehime
2003

PATCHWORK MEMORIES

Quilts *with the* Charm *of* Yesteryear

Retta Warehime

Martingale®
& COMPANY

Patchwork Memories:
Quilts with the Charm of Yesteryear
© 2003 Retta Warehime

That Patchwork Place® is an imprint
of Martingale & Company®.

Martingale & Company
20205 144th Avenue NE
Woodinville, WA 98072-8478
www.martingale-pub.com

Printed in China
08 07 06 05 04 03   8 7 6 5 4 3 2 1

Library of Congress Cataloging-in-Publication Data

Warehime, Retta.
   Patchwork memories : quilts with the charm of yesteryear / Retta Warehime.
      p. cm.
   ISBN 1-56477-513-5
   1. Patchwork—Patterns. 2. Quilting—Patterns.
I. Title.
   TT835 . W3568 2003
   746.46—dc21

                                        2003013773

~~~~~~~~~~~~~~~~~~~~~~~~~~~

MISSION STATEMENT
Dedicated to providing quality products
and service to inspire creativity.

~~~~~~~~~~~~~~~~~~~~~~~~~~~

~~~~~~ CREDITS ~~~~~~

President ～ Nancy J. Martin
CEO ～ Daniel J. Martin
Publisher ～ Jane Hamada
Editorial Director ～ Mary V. Green
Managing Editor ～ Tina Cook
Technical Editor ～ Ellen Pahl
Copy Editor ～ Karen Koll
Design Director ～ Stan Green
Illustrator ～ Laurel Strand
Text Designer ～ Regina Girard
Cover Designer ～ Stan Green
Photographer ～ Brent Kane

~ Dedication ~

To all the beautiful, courageous children at Children's Hospital and Regional Medical Center in Seattle, Washington.

To my own four beautiful children and two grandchildren, who have been blessed with good health: Shawna, Jayme, Marci, Gregg, Whitney, and Cole.

~ Acknowledgments ~

To my family and friends who always support and encourage me, I truly appreciate your unwavering enthusiasm that continues with every quilt I design.

To Pam Clarke, professional quilting artist, thank you for enhancing the quilts with your beautiful workmanship and design.

Kim Penttila graciously helped me out at the last minute with her computer knowledge.

Thanks go to my editor, Ellen Pahl, for polishing my manuscript and checking the quilt instructions.

I am very grateful to Mary Green, Karen Soltys, Terry Martin, and photographer Brent Kane (especially for his "Quilter Filter"), and the rest of the Martingale staff for taking my book ideas and making them a reality!

Thanks to the Jarvis family of Woodinville, Washington, for letting us photograph the quilts in their lovely home.

And thank you to all the authors and narrators of audio books I listen to while I design, sew, and quilt. They keep me inspired and focused on the task at hand.

Contents

Introduction

It's not unusual for people who love quilts to also love antiques and collectibles. I am one of those quilters who is passionate not only about quilts, but about all things antique, vintage, or charmingly old. I have a penchant for antique furniture of all kinds, repainting and restoring it for my home. I collect vintage dishtowels, tins, roosters, baskets, and redware. I pair my collections with my quilts and have quilts hanging all through the house. I do favor darker colors, and they go well with my collections.

The quilts in this book are perfect to use in your home to complement antiques and collections of any type. Choose a pattern, then choose fabrics in colors that coordinate or complement your prized possessions. They will work with just about any country style or Early American look. If you've been collecting some of those wonderful reproduction fabrics or authentic vintage fabrics, one of the quilts in this book will undoubtedly be inspiration for you to create a wonderful quilt with them.

Patchwork Memories is written for all quilters, from beginner to advanced. The projects are easy to piece even though they may look complex. I always use speedy and accurate piecing techniques to ensure that I am able to finish projects quickly and successfully. If you are new to quilting, I suggest that you read "Quiltmaking Essentials," beginning on page 66, to get started on the right foot.

I feel that making quilts is a way to create a link from the present to the past as well as to the future. Last year I decided that I wanted each member of my family and all my good friends to have one of my original quilts. I have made each of the quilts in this book for someone special in my life as a way of sharing a treasured part of my life with each one of them. I encourage you to look through the book, choose your favorite quilt, and get busy. Make a quilt and make that connection to the past and future. Pass on the passion and create your own patchwork memories.

Granddad's Shirts

Finished Quilt: 44" x 68"

Finished Blocks: 8" and 4"

I love black and tan, and I had been collecting black and tan fabrics for years. I designed this quilt around my collection and used up a good portion of it. I paired my fabrics with a background that is a reproduction shirting fabric. Men's shirts were made of fabrics like these in the late 1800s, and reproductions are readily available today. I didn't add any borders to this quilt; quilters in the past often didn't have large enough pieces of fabric to add traditional borders. Can't you just picture this quilt draped over a vintage oak rocker or hung on the wall near a grandfather clock?

Materials

Yardages are based on 42"-wide fabrics unless otherwise noted.

9 fat quarters of assorted blacks and tans for blocks*

1⅜ yards of light print for sashing rectangles

1⅜ yards of light print or scraps for block background

3⅛ yards of fabric for backing

⅝ yard of fabric for binding

50" x 74" piece of batting

Choose a variety of dark and medium dark fabrics.

Cutting

From the fat quarters, cut:
38 strips, 1½" x 20"
14 strips, 2½" x 20"

From the block background fabric, cut:
16 strips, 1½" x 20"
17 strips, 2½" x 20"
3 strips, 2½" x 42"; cut into 48 squares, 2½" x 2½"

From the sashing fabric, cut:
5 strips, 8½" x 42"; cut into 38 rectangles, 8½" x 4½"

From the binding fabric, cut:
6 strips, 2½" x 42"

Block I and II Assembly

Blocks I and II are made from segments cut from five different strip sets. Assemble the strip sets, referring to the diagrams below for color placement. Randomly place the black and tan strips, but position the background strips specifically where shown. Press all the seam allowances in the direction of the arrows on the diagrams.

1. Sew together strips cut from fat quarters as shown to make four of strip set A. Cut 48 segments, 1½" wide.

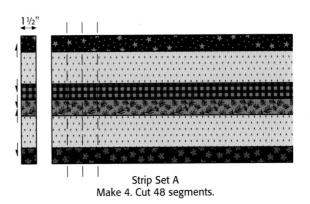

Strip Set A
Make 4. Cut 48 segments.

Designed and pieced by Retta Warehime, quilted by Pam Clarke. This quilt will be given to my daughter Jayme Gilbert, so I can visit my black and tan fabric collection whenever I want.

2. Sew strips together as shown to make six of strip set B. Cut 48 segments, 2½" wide.

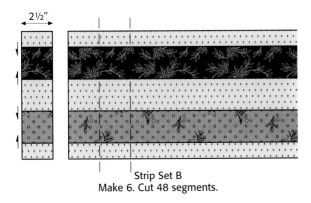

Strip Set B
Make 6. Cut 48 segments.

3. Sew strips together as shown to make eight of strip set C. Cut 96 segments, 1½" wide.

Strip Set C
Make 8. Cut 96 segments.

4. Sew strips together as shown to make three of strip set D. Cut 30 segments, 1½" wide.

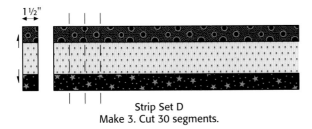

Strip Set D
Make 3. Cut 30 segments.

5. Sew strips together as shown to make two of strip set E. Cut 15 segments, 2½" wide.

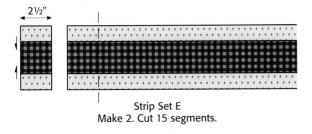

Strip Set E
Make 2. Cut 15 segments.

6. Assemble 24 of block I using segments A, B, C, and the 2½" background squares.

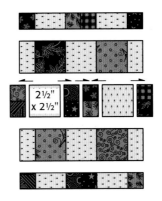

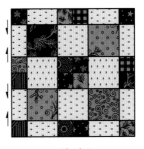

Block I
Make 24.

7. Assemble 15 of block II using segments D and E.

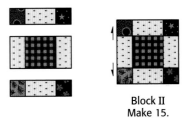

Block II
Make 15.

Remarks from Retta

I think this quilt would also look fabulous in reds and blacks with a shirting background. Or, try indigos with red for a patriotic version.

Assembly and Finishing

1. Alternate four of block I and three sashing rectangles to make a row. Press toward the sashing. Make six rows. Make five rows alternating three of block II and four sashing rectangles. Press toward the sashing.

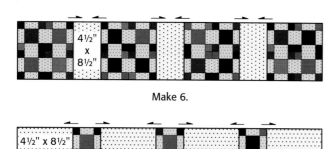

Make 6.

Make 5.

2. Join the rows together. Press toward the block II rows.

3. Piece and trim the backing fabric so it is approximately 6" larger than the quilt top.

4. Layer the quilt top with the batting and backing; baste. Quilt as desired.

5. Refer to "Finishing" on page 77 for details if needed. Trim the batting and backing so the edges are even with the quilt top. Bind the quilt and add a label.

Crystal Kaleidoscope

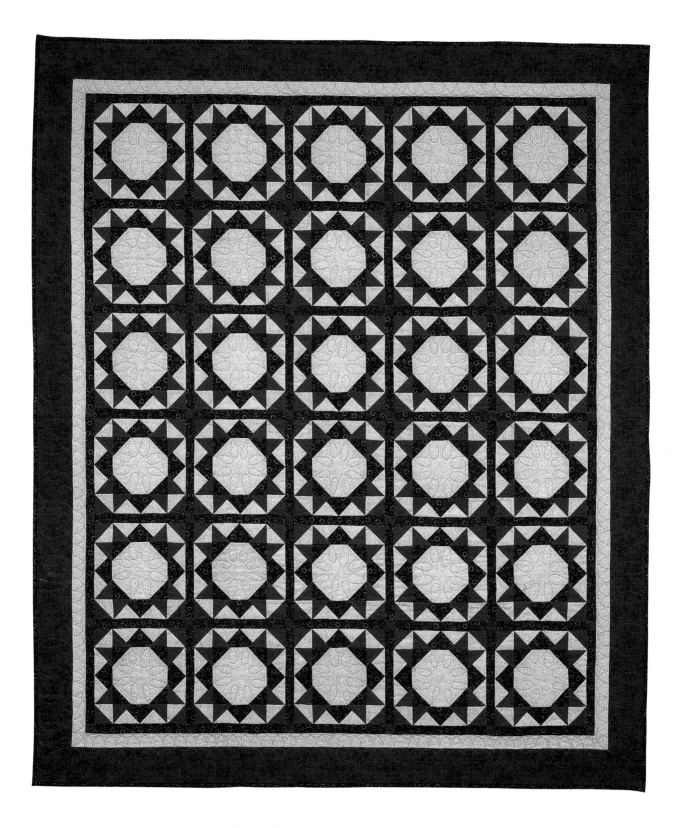

Designed and pieced by Retta Warehime, quilted by Pam Clarke.
My daughter Shawna chose this quilt to hang in her family room during the Christmas season.
She sometimes swaps it with other seasonal quilts during the year.

Finished Quilt: 67" x 78"

Finished Block: 10"

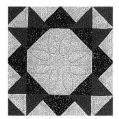

This classic quilt looks far more complicated than it really is. The blocks are all made with squares and rectangles; you won't have to cut a single triangle! I made this quilt out of very sweet, old-fashioned-looking prints in a traditional red-and-green color scheme. It can be used for holiday decorating or displayed year-round with your favorite antiques. Fold it over a quilt rack, hang it on the wall, or use it on the guest bed. It will look wonderful anywhere.

Materials

Yardages are based on 42"-wide fabrics.

3⅝ yards of light green print for block background and inner border

3 yards of green print for blocks

1⅞ yards of red print 1 for blocks

1⅛ yards of red print 2 for outer border

4¾ yards of fabric for backing

¾ yard of fabric for binding

73" x 84" piece of batting

Cutting

From light green print, cut:

7 strips, 2" x 42"

5 strips, 3" x 42"; cut into 60 squares, 3" x 3"

15 strips, 3½" x 42"; cut into 240 rectangles, 2½" x 3½"

5 strips, 6½" x 42"; cut into 30 squares, 6½" x 6½"

From red print 1, cut:

1 strip, 1½" x 42"; cut into 7 squares, 1½" x 1½"

2 strips, 1½" x 42"

15 strips, 2½" x 42"; cut into 240 squares, 2½" x 2½"

5 strips, 3" x 42"; cut into 60 squares, 3" x 3"

From green print, cut:

8 strips, 2½" x 42"; cut into 120 squares, 2½" x 2½"

8 strips, 4½" x 42"; cut into 120 rectangles, 4½" x 2½"

2 strips, 10½" x 42"

2 strips, 10½" x 42"; cut into 36 strips, 1½" x 10½"

From red print 2, cut:

7 strips, 4½" x 42"

From binding fabric, cut:

8 strips, 2½" x 42"

Block Assembly

1. Using a pencil and a ruler, draw a diagonal line from corner to corner on the back of all the 3" light green background squares. Position each light green square on top of a 3" red square, right sides together. Stitch ¼" away from the marked line on both sides. Cut on the marked line. Press seams toward the red fabric. Trim and square up the half-square-triangle units to 2½" x 2½" (refer to "Squaring Up Blocks" on page 72). Make 120.

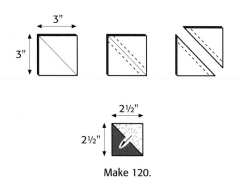

Make 120.

2. Position one 2½" x 3½" light green print rectangle on top of a 4½" x 2½" green print rectangle, right sides together, matching left edges as shown. Draw a diagonal line from the corner of the rectangle underneath to the corner of the rectangle on top. Stitch on the drawn line. Trim seam to ¼" from the stitching; press seam toward the light green. Repeat on the right side to make unit A. Make 120.

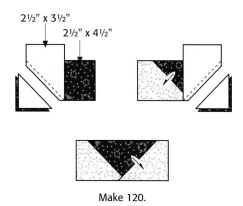

Make 120.

3. Position one 2½" red square on top of each end of the 120 A units right sides together. Draw a diagonal line as shown and stitch on the line. Trim seam to ¼" from the stitching; press toward the red.

Unit A
Make 120.

4. Join the half-square-triangle units made in step 1 to each end of 60 A units to make 60 of unit B. Press toward the half-square-triangle units.

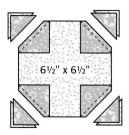

Unit B
Make 60.

5. Position one 2½" green print square on each corner of a 6½" light green print square, right sides together, matching all edges as shown. Draw a diagonal line and stitch on the line. Trim seam to ¼" from the stitching; press seams toward the light green. Make 30 of these center squares.

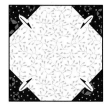

Make 30.

6. Sew an A unit to each side of the center squares. Press.

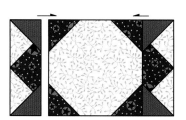

7. Sew a B unit to the top and bottom. Press.

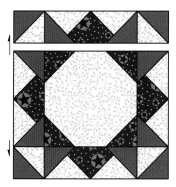

Assembly and Finishing

1. Sew each of the 1½" x 42" red strips to a 10½" x 42" green strip to make two strip sets. Cut the strip sets into 35 segments, 1½" wide.

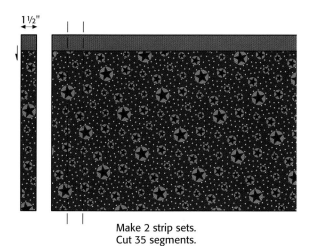

1½"

Make 2 strip sets.
Cut 35 segments.

2. Join five segments from step 1 and one additional 1½" red square to make seven sashing rows.

Make 7.

3. Make six rows of five blocks and six 1½" x 10½" green strips as shown. Press toward the sashing.

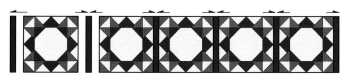

Make 6.

4. Join the six rows of blocks with the seven sashing rows. Press toward the sashing rows.

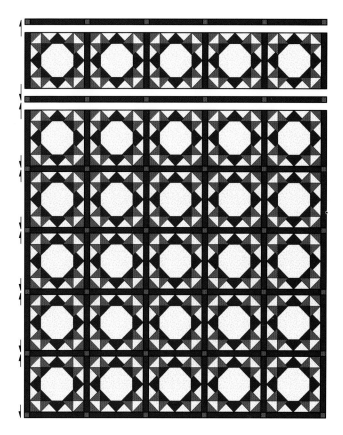

5. Referring to "Borders" on page 74, piece, measure, and trim the light green print inner-border strips and sew them to the side edges of the quilt top first, and then to the top and bottom edges. Repeat for the red print 2 outer borders.

6. Piece and trim the backing fabric so it is approximately 6" larger than the quilt top.

7. Layer the quilt with the batting and backing; baste. Quilt as desired. The open areas of the blocks are perfect for a floral or feathered wreath design.

8. Refer to "Finishing" on page 77 for details if needed. Trim the batting and backing fabric so the edges are even with the quilt top.

9. Bind the quilt and add a label.

Star Echoes

Finished Quilt: 43" x 60"
Finished Blocks: 12"

I love how the green echo of the larger star block in this quilt almost looks like a blossoming flower. I've paired traditional red and green in small-scale, reproduction prints, making this quilt a perfect accessory for a collection of ironstone china, red transferware, or even vintage toys. You can achieve a completely different look, depending on your fabric choices.

Materials

Yardages are based on 42"-wide fabrics.

1⅝ yards of light print for background

1¼ yards of red print 1 for Star block points and outer border

1 yard of green print 1 for Star blocks

⅞ yard of green print 2 for accent border and binding

¼ yard of red print 2 for block centers

2⅞ yards of fabric for backing

49" x 66" piece of batting

Cutting

From light print, cut:
2 strips, 2½" x 42"
3 strips, 2½" x 42"; cut into 8 squares, 2½" x 2½";
    4 rectangles, 2½" x 8½"; and 4 rectangles,
    2½" x 12½"
2 strips, 4½" x 42"; cut into 32 rectangles,
    2½" x 4½"
2 squares, 9½" x 9½"; cut once on the diagonal for
    corner triangles
2 squares, 18½" x 18½"; cut twice on the diagonal
    for side setting triangles

From green print 1, cut:
2 strips, 2½" x 42"
4 strips, 2½" x 42"; cut into 64 squares, 2½" x 2½"
3 strips, 4½" x 42"; cut into 48 rectangles,
    2½" x 4½"

From red print 1, cut:
3 strips, 2½" x 42"; cut into 48 squares, 2½" x 2½"
8 strips, 3¾" x 42"

From red print 2, cut:
1 strip, 4½" x 42"; cut into 8 squares, 4½" x 4½"

From green print 2, cut:
5 strips, 1¾" x 42"
6 strips, 2½" x 42"

Designed and pieced by Retta Warehime, quilted by Pam Clarke.
This quilt is for Terry Burkhart, who loves red and green.

Block A and B Assembly

1. Assemble two strip sets using the 2½" x 42" green print 1 and light print strips. Cut into 24 segments, 2½" wide.

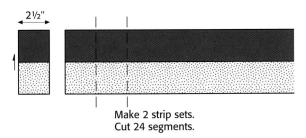

Make 2 strip sets.
Cut 24 segments.

2. Make 12 of unit A and 12 of unit B using the 2½" segments and the 2½" x 4½" green print 1 rectangles.

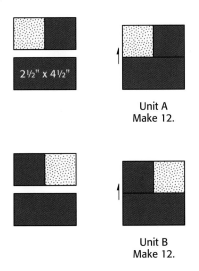

Unit A
Make 12.

Unit B
Make 12.

3. Using a pencil and ruler, draw a diagonal line from corner to corner on the wrong side of all the 2½" green print 1 squares. Position each green square on top of a 2½" x 4½" light print rectangle, right sides together, matching left edges as shown. Stitch on the drawn line. Trim the seam to ¼" from the stitching; press toward the green. Repeat for the right side to make unit C. Make 32.

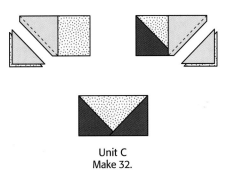

Unit C
Make 32.

4. Using the same method as in step 3, sew a 2½" red print 1 square to each side of a 2½" x 4½" green print 1 rectangle to make unit D. Make 24.

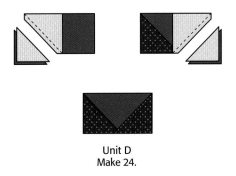

Unit D
Make 24.

5. Sew unit C to the top of unit D as shown. Make 24 of unit C-D.

Unit C-D
Make 24.

6. To make block A, arrange units A, B, and C-D with the 4½" red print 2 center square as shown. Sew the units together in rows; sew the rows together to make the block. Press. Make six of block A.

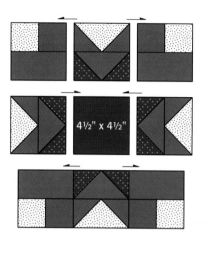

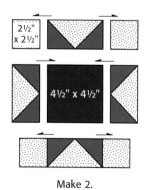

Block A
Make 6.

7. To make block B, arrange four of unit C, four 2½" light print squares and the 4½" red print 2 center square as shown. Sew the units together in rows; press. Sew the rows together to make the block. Make two.

Make 2.

8. Sew 2½" x 8½" light print rectangles to the top and bottom of each star unit from step 7. Press toward the light print. Sew the 2½" x 12½" light print rectangles to each side. Press. Make two of block B.

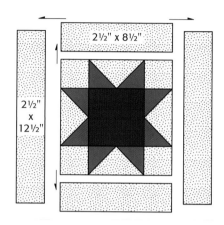

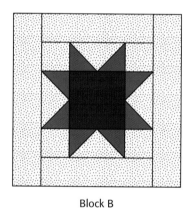

Block B
Make 2.

Remarks from Retta

If you set the blocks straight instead of on the diagonal and use sashing between the blocks, you will have an entirely different quilt.

Assembly and Finishing

1. Arrange the blocks and setting triangles into diagonal rows, alternating blocks A and B. Sew the blocks and side setting triangles together. Add the corner triangles last.

2. Measuring ¼" from the points of the block, trim the outside edges of the quilt.

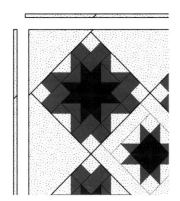

Trim ¼" from points.

3. Referring to "Borders" on page 74, measure and trim the 1¾" x 42" green print 2 accent-border strips and sew them to the sides of the quilt top first, and then to the top and bottom. Repeat for the red print 1 outer borders.

4. Piece and trim the backing fabric so it is approximately 6" larger than the quilt top.

5. Layer the quilt top with the batting and backing; baste. Quilt as desired.

6. Refer to "Finishing" on page 77 for details if needed. Trim the batting and backing so the edges are even with the quilt top. Bind the quilt and add a label.

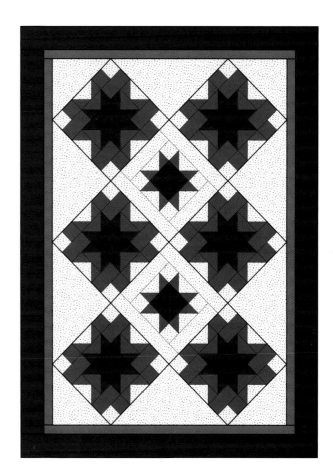

Licorice Twist

Finished Quilt: 50" x 60"

Finished Block: 10"

All my life I have twisted red and black licorice together before I eat it. Anyone who knows me will relate to the design and name of this quilt. This is another quilt in which I opted not to add borders; this creates a vintage look at the outset. I also chose fabrics that lend it the charm of yesteryear. This striking quilt will serve as a fabulous accent almost anywhere in your home. It would look especially appealing displayed with a collection of antique game boards.

Materials

Yardages are based on 42"-wide fabrics.

2⅝ yards of light print for background

1 yard of red print for blocks

1 yard of black print for blocks

3⅜ yards of fabric for backing

⅝ yard of fabric for binding

56" x 66" piece of batting

Cutting

From red print, cut:
6 strips, 2½" x 42"; cut into 90 squares, 2½" x 2½"
2 strips, 6½" x 42"; cut into 30 rectangles, 2½" x 6½"

From black print, cut:
6 strips, 2½" x 42"; cut into 90 squares, 2½" x 2½"
2 strips, 6½" x 42"; cut into 30 rectangles, 2½" x 6½"

From light print, cut:
4 strips, 2½" x 42"; cut into 60 squares, 2½" x 2½"
6 strips, 6½" x 42"; cut into 90 rectangles, 2½" x 6½"
4 strips, 8½" x 42"; cut into 60 rectangles, 2½" x 8½"

From binding fabric, cut:
6 strips, 2½" x 42"

Designed and pieced by Retta Warehime, quilted by Pam Clarke. This quilt is for my longtime friend Colleen Medchill, who still (after 30 years) sends me black and red licorice for my birthday.

Block Assembly

1. Using a pencil and a ruler, draw a diagonal line from corner to corner on the wrong side of all the 2½" black and red squares. Position the squares on top of the light print rectangles as shown, right sides together. Sew on the marked line and trim the seam allowance to ¼". Follow the illustrations to make units A through E for the blocks.

2. Arrange units A through E with the black 2½" x 6½" rectangles, red 2½" x 6½" rectangles, and the light print 2½" squares as shown. Sew together in rows and press. Sew the rows together to make 30 blocks. Press 15 blocks with the seam allowances away from center and 15 blocks with the seams toward the center.

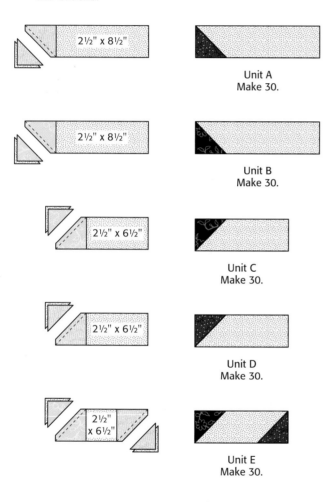

Unit A
Make 30.

Unit B
Make 30.

Unit C
Make 30.

Unit D
Make 30.

Unit E
Make 30.

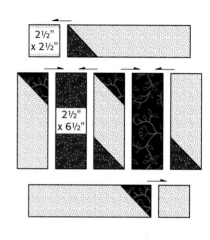

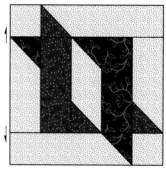

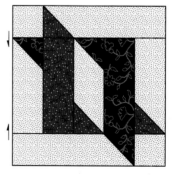

Make 15.

Make 15.

~~~~~~~~~~~~~~~~~~~~~~~~~~~~~~

Remarks from Retta

I like to use a white Chaco Liner to mark the diagonal lines on dark fabrics. It shows up well and makes a sharp, fine line. I use fine-point permanent ink for light fabrics (I like the Pigma .01 marker).

~~~~~~~~~~~~~~~~~~~~~~~~~~~~~~

Assembly and Finishing

1. Arrange the blocks in six rows of five blocks each, with all the blocks going in the same direction. Position the blocks according to the pressing direction so that you will have opposing seams. Sew the blocks together and press in opposite directions from row to row. Join the rows and press all the seams in one direction.

2. Piece and trim the backing fabric so it is approximately 6" larger than the quilt top.

3. Layer the quilt top with the batting and backing; baste. Quilt as desired.

4. Refer to "Finishing" on page 77 for details if needed. Trim the batting and backing so the edges are even with the quilt top. Bind the quilt and add a label.

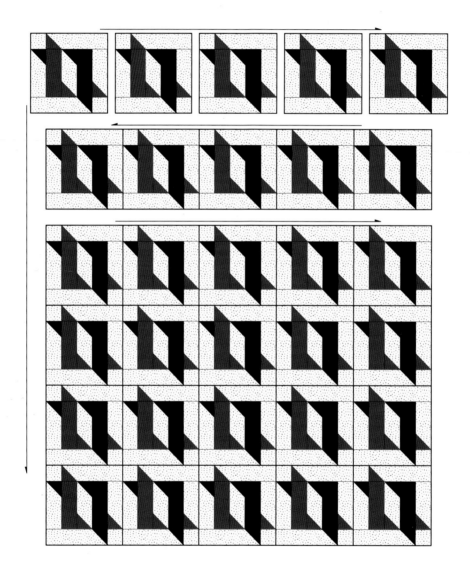

Greggory's Quilt

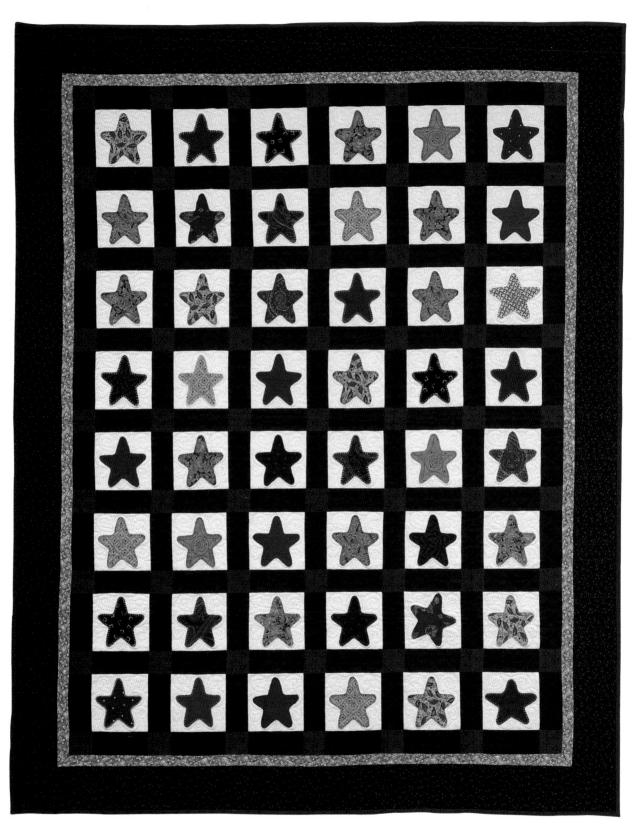

Designed and pieced by Retta Warehime, quilted by Pam Clarke.
This quilt was started for my son, Gregg, before he was born (that's when I appliquéd
the stars to the background squares). Sixteen years later he has his completed quilt!

Finished Quilt: 54" x 68"

Finished Block: 5"

Stars have a perennial appeal, practically guaranteed to stir up memories of childhood and pleasant afternoons spent drawing stars, or evenings looking up at the sky. You can make these stars in any colors or fabrics to use up your scraps. This charming quilt is a perfect take-along project when you have a few minutes to stitch. The blocks are small, and the stars are appliquéd by hand with a blanket stitch. After all the blocks are finished, simply sash it together. Drape this quilt on a sofa or stuffed chair to cuddle up in when you're relaxing or reading.

Materials

Yardages are based on 42"-wide fabrics unless otherwise noted.

2¼ yards of black print 1 for sashing

1¼ yards of white-on-white print for block background

1 yard of red print for corner squares and binding

⅞ yard of black print 2 for outer border

⅜ yard of blue-gray print for inner border

48 squares, 5" x 5", or scraps for stars*

3½ yards of fabric for backing

60" x 74" piece of batting

2¼ yards of lightweight fusible web for fusible appliqué

Template plastic (optional)

Embroidery floss for hand blanket stitching

Note: If you want all the stars to be cut from the same fabric, purchase 1 yard.

Cutting

From white-on-white print, cut:
7 strips, 5½" x 42"; cut into 48 squares, 5½" x 5½"

From red print, cut:
11 strips, 2½" x 42"
9 squares, 2½" x 2½"

From black print 1, cut:
4 strips, 5½" x 42"
4 strips, 5½" x 42"; cut into 56 rectangles, 2½" x 5½"

From blue-gray print, cut:
6 strips, 1½" x 42"

From black print 2, cut:
6 strips, 4½" x 42"

Block Assembly

Note: Use your favorite appliqué method to complete the Star blocks. The quilt shown was made using lightweight fusible web with a hand blanket-stitch. I used two strands of embroidery floss. (See "Appliqué Basics" on page 69 for further details.)

Prepare the stars, using the pattern on page 35. Center the stars on the white-on-white squares and appliqué in place.

Make 48.

Assembly and Finishing

1. Using four 2½" x 42" red print strips and the 5½" x 42" black print 1 strips, make two strip sets as shown. Cut into 27 segments, 2½" wide.

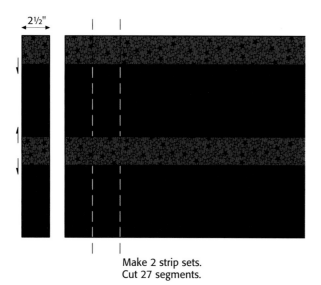

2½"

Make 2 strip sets.
Cut 27 segments.

2. Sew three segments from step 1 together; add a 2½" red square to the end. Make nine sashing rows.

Make 9.

3. Make eight rows using six appliquéd blocks and seven black print 1 rectangles in each. Press toward sashing.

2½" x 5½"

Make 8.

4. Join the eight rows of blocks with the sashing rows. Press toward the sashing.

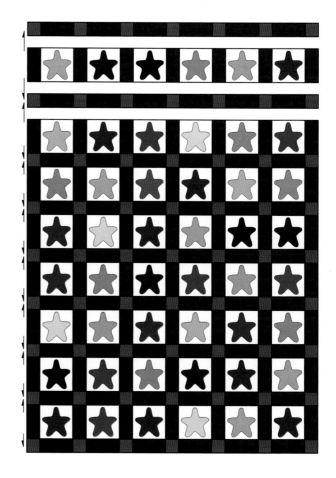

5. Referring to "Borders" on page 74, piece, measure, and trim the blue-gray print strips and sew them to the sides of the quilt and the top and bottom of the quilt top. Repeat for the 4½" black print 2 outer borders.

6. Piece and trim the backing fabric so it is approximately 6" larger than the quilt top.

7. Layer the quilt with the batting and backing; baste. Quilt as desired.

8. Refer to "Finishing" on page 77 for details if needed. Trim the batting and backing fabric so the edges are even with the quilt top.

9. Bind the quilt and add a label.

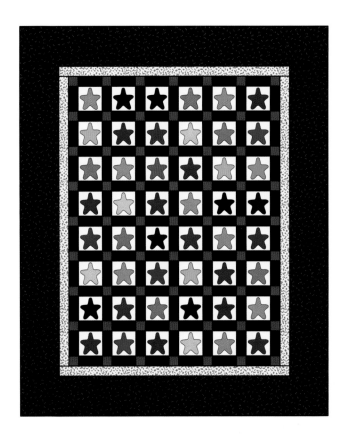

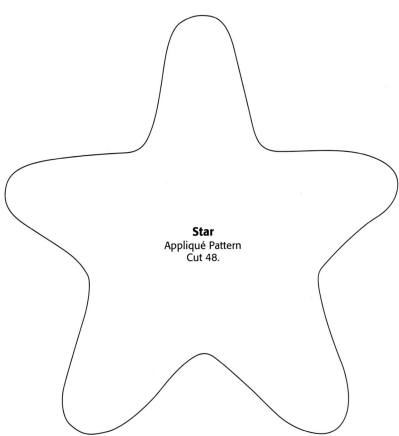

Star
Appliqué Pattern
Cut 48.

Note: For hand appliqué,
add ¼" seam allowance for turn-under.

Simply Stars

Finished Quilt: 61" x 74"

Finished Block: 12"

I absolutely love Star blocks. I wanted to make a star that was simple, but different. This design fits the bill. The block is actually a nine-patch, and it goes together very quickly. The quilt looks more complicated than it really is. It is sized for a twin bed and would look right at home with just about any style bed, from a vintage iron bed to a wooden spindle bed frame. And of course it's lovely on a table, too.

Materials

Yardages are based on 42"-wide fabrics.

4¼ yards of tan print for background

2⅛ yards of blue print for stars and sashing

¾ yard of black solid for corner squares and binding

3⅞ yards of fabric for backing

67" x 80" piece of batting

Cutting

From blue print, cut:

15 strips, 2½" x 42"; cut into 240 squares, 2½" x 2½"

19 strips, 1½" x 42"; cut into 22 rectangles, 1½" x 2½", and 49 strips, 1½" x 12½"

From tan print, cut:

7 strips, 2½" x 42"; cut into 18 rectangles, 2½" x 12½", and 4 rectangles, 2½" x 4½"

7 strips, 2½" x 42"

23 strips, 4½" x 42"; cut into 180 squares, 4½" x 4½"

From black solid, cut:

2 strips, 1½" x 2½"; cut into 30 squares, 1½" x 1½"

7 strips, 2½" x 42"

Block Assembly

1. Using a pencil and a ruler, draw a diagonal line from corner to corner on the wrong side of all the 2½" blue squares. Position a blue square on top of a 4½" tan print square, right sides together, matching lower left edges as shown. Stitch on the drawn line. Trim the seam to ¼"; press toward the blue print. Make 160 of unit A.

Unit A
Make 160.

Remarks from Retta

Use a light-color quilter's marking pencil or a Chaco Liner so that the diagonal line shows up well when marking on the dark fabric.

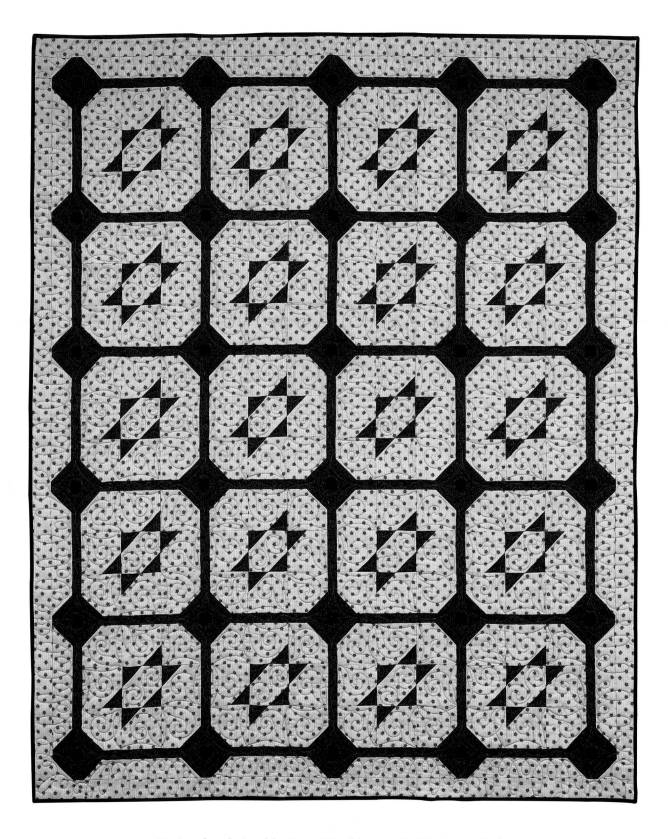

Designed and pieced by Retta Warehime, quilted by Pam Clarke.
This quilt was made for my daughter Marci Warehime, who uses and
enjoys it in her dormitory at the University of Washington.

2. Using the same method as in step 1, sew two 2½" blue squares to opposite corners of a 4½" tan print square. Make 20 of unit B.

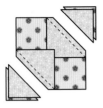

Unit B
Make 20.

3. Arrange units A and B in rows as shown. Make 40 of the unit A rows and 20 of the unit A and B rows. Press.

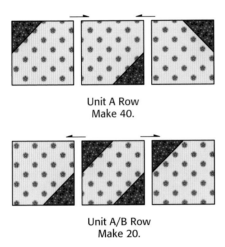

Unit A Row
Make 40.

Unit A/B Row
Make 20.

4. Assemble the rows made in step 3 into 20 Star blocks. Press.

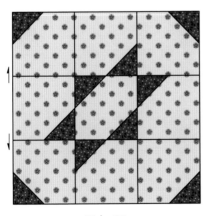

Make 20.

Assembly and Finishing

1. Make five rows of four blocks and five 1½" x 12½" sashing strips each.

1½"
x 12½"

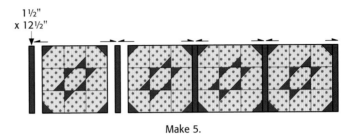

Make 5.

2. Make six rows of four blue strips and five black squares each. Join the block rows with the sashing rows. Press.

1½" x 12½"

Make 6.

3. Using the remaining blue squares and the tan print rectangles, make 2 of unit C, 2 of unit D, and 18 of unit E as shown in the diagram below.

2½" x 4½"

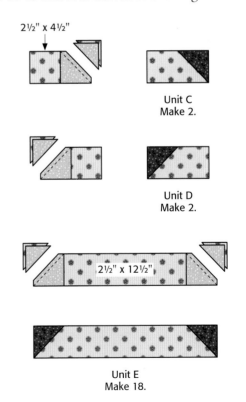

Unit C
Make 2.

Unit D
Make 2.

2½" x 12½"

Unit E
Make 18.

4. Assemble two side borders using five of unit E and six blue rectangles. Sew to the sides of the quilt top.

Side Border
Make 2.

5. Referring to "Borders" on page 74, piece, measure, and trim the tan print strips and sew two to the sides of the quilt top.

6. Assemble two borders for the top and bottom, using units C, D, E, and the blue rectangles. Sew to the top and bottom of the quilt.

Top or Bottom Border
Make 2.

7. Sew tan print strips to the top and bottom of the quilt.

8. Piece and trim the backing fabric so it is approximately 6" larger than the quilt top.

9. Layer the quilt with the batting and backing; baste. Quilt as desired.

10. Refer to "Finishing" on page 77 for details if needed. Trim the batting and backing fabric so the edges are even with the quilt top.

11. Bind the quilt and add a label.

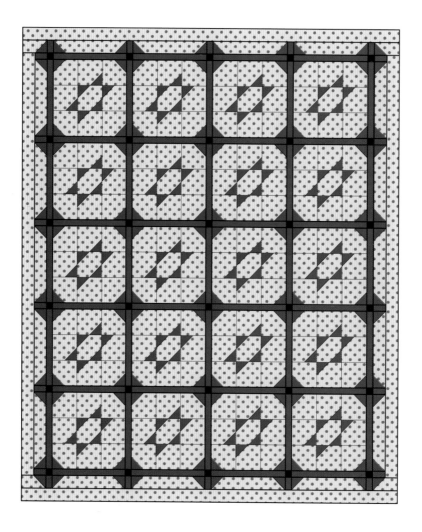

Autumn Lily

Designed and pieced by Retta Warehime, quilted by Pam Clarke.
"Autumn Lily" will be donated to Children's Hospital and Regional Medical Center
in Seattle, Washington, for sale in a fundraising auction.

Finished Quilt: 67½" x 82½"

Finished Block: 7½"

This striking quilt is made from dark, medium, and light fall colors, combined with scrappy backgrounds. The stem of the lily is appliquéd in place and adds a subtle three-dimensional effect. Try this in red and green fabrics to achieve the look of a Christmas lily. If you have scraps on hand, this quilt will help you use them up. I've set the lily blocks in a staggered, asymmetric fashion. I think it makes the quilt unique and more interesting. The quilt will fit a twin bed, but you can also hang it on a wall behind a piece of antique furniture for a memorable impression.

Materials

Yardages are based on 42"-wide fabrics.

4 yards total or scraps of light prints for background*

1½ yards *each* of gold, tan, brown, and red prints for Flower and border blocks*

1 yard total of green prints for leaves and outer border

⅜ yard of green print for stem

¼ yard of brown print for stem bottom

5¼ yards of fabric for backing

¾ yard of fabric for binding

74" x 89" piece of batting

***Note:** Use several different light fabrics for the backgrounds and a variety of darks, mediums, and lights in gold, tan, brown, and red for the blocks. Total yardage is given. Remember that dark, medium, and light are relative, and depend on the fabrics you place together. For example, when a medium is next to a light, the medium becomes a dark.*

Cutting

From light prints, cut:

5 strips, 2½" x 42"; cut into 75 squares, 2½" x 2½"

11 strips, 1½" x 42"; cut into 60 rectangles, 3" x 1½", and 60 rectangles, 4" x 1½"

2 strips, 4½" x 42"; cut into 30 rectangles, 4½" x 2½"

4 strips, 5" x 42"; cut into 30 squares, 5" x 5". Cut the squares in half diagonally once.

3 strips, 7½" x 42"; cut into 15 squares, 7½" x 7½". Cut the squares in half diagonally once.

4 strips, 8" x 42"; cut into 29 rectangles, 8" x 4¼"

6 squares, 4¼" x 4¼"

4 squares, 4⅝" x 4⅝"

Continued on next page

From gold, tan, brown, and red prints, cut:**

2 dark strips total, 2½" x 42"; cut into 25 squares, 2½" x 2½"

2 medium strips total, 2½" x 42"; cut into: 25 squares, 2½" x 2½"

2 light strips total, 2½" x 42"; cut into 25 squares, 2½" x 2½"

2 dark strips total, 3" x 21"; cut into 10 squares, 3" x 3"

2 medium strips total, 3" x 21"; cut into 10 squares, 3" x 3"

2 light strips total, 3" x 21"; cut into 10 squares, 3" x 3"

3 dark strips total, 4¼" x 42"; cut into 20 squares, 4¼" x 4¼"

4 medium strips total, 4¼" x 42"; cut into 36 squares, 4¼" x 4¼"

2 light strips total, 4¼" x 42"; cut into 16 squares, 4¼" x 4¼"

7 dark strips total, 4⅝" x 42"; cut into 47 squares, 4⅝" x 4⅝"

6 medium strips total, 4⅝" x 42"; cut into 47 squares, 4⅝" x 4⅝"

5 light strips total, 4⅝" x 42"; cut into 34 squares, 4⅝" x 4⅝"

From green stem print, cut:

5 strips, 1¼" x 42"

From green prints for leaves and outer border, cut:

7 strips, 1½" x 42"; cut into 60 rectangles, 1½" x 1¾", and 60 rectangles, 2¾" x 1½"

1 strip, 4⅝" x 42"; cut into 8 squares, 4⅝" x 4⅝"

1 strip, 4¼" x 42"; cut into 9 squares, 4¼" x 4¼"

4 strips, 2½" x 42"; cut into 60 squares, 2½" x 2½"

From brown print, cut:

1 strip, 2¼" x 42"; cut into 15 squares, 2¼" x 2¼". Cut the squares diagonally once.

From the binding fabric, cut:

8 strips, 2½" x 42"

** You may want to cut strips into 21" lengths from a larger variety of colors to achieve a scrappier look. Don't forget you can use the wrong side of the fabric, too.

Block Assembly

1. Using a pencil and a ruler, draw a diagonal line from corner to corner on the wrong side of all the 2½" light print squares. Position each light print square on top of the dark, medium, and light 2½" squares cut from the gold, tans, browns, and reds, right sides together. Stitch ¼" from each side of the marked lines. Cut on the marked lines. Press seams toward the darker fabric. Trim and square up the half-square-triangle units to 1¾" (refer to "Squaring Up Blocks" on page 72).

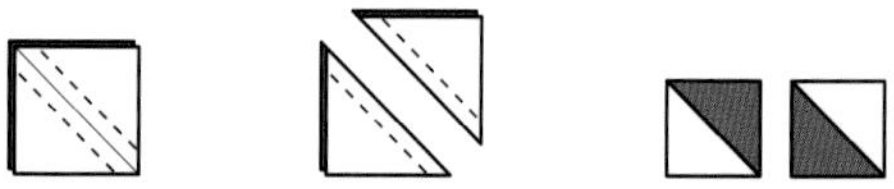

Make 150.

2. Sew 60 half-square-triangle units together in pairs, and 90 together in groups of three as shown. Make 30 of each.

Make 30.   Make 30.

3. Sew units of two half-square-triangles to one side of each of the 3" dark, medium, and light squares. Then sew the units of three half-square-triangles to the other side. This portion of the Flower block measures 4¼" square. Make 30.

 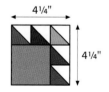

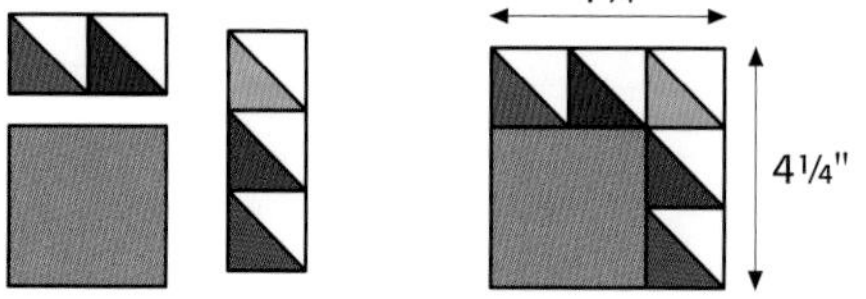

Make 30.

4. Sew a 5" light print triangle to each of two sides of the 4¼" Flower block as shown. Align a 6" x 12" ruler ¼" from the intersecting triangle seams, with the 45° angle along the side of the Flower block, and trim ¼" away from the point.

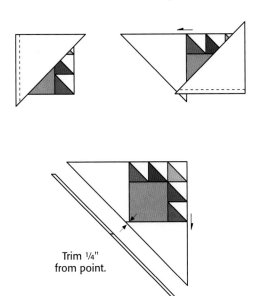

Trim ¼"
from point.

5. Fold the 1¼" stem strips in half lengthwise with wrong sides together. Sew a ¼" seam down the long side, using a short stitch length. Trim the seam allowance to ⅛" inch. Cut into 30 stems, 6" long. Press the seams open with the seam centered; that will be the wrong side of the stem.

Trim.→

6. Center and pin one 6" stem piece, with the seam to the back, on a 4½" x 2½" light print rectangle. To make the center leaf units, position a green 2½" square on the left side corner of the background rectangle, right sides together, matching raw edges. Draw a diagonal line and stitch on the line. Trim the seam to ¼"; press the seam toward the green. Repeat for the right side. Press toward the green.

Pin.
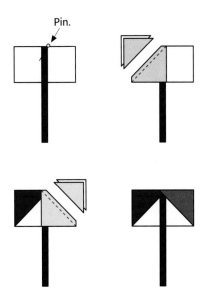

7. Refer to the diagrams below for color placement and size; assemble 30 each of the right and left upper-leaf units. Press toward the leaves.

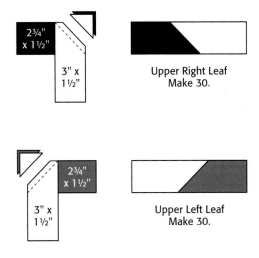

2¾"
x 1½"

3" x
1½"

Upper Right Leaf
Make 30.

3" x
1½"

2¾"
x 1½"

Upper Left Leaf
Make 30.

8. Refer to the diagrams below for color placement and size; assemble 30 each of the right and left lower-leaf units. Press toward the leaves.

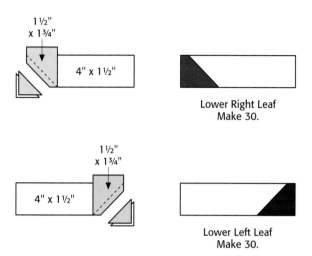

1½" x 1¾"

4" x 1½"

Lower Right Leaf
Make 30.

1½" x 1¾"

4" x 1½"

Lower Left Leaf
Make 30.

9. Sew the right upper- and lower-leaf units together as shown, and then sew the left upper- and lower-leaf units together.

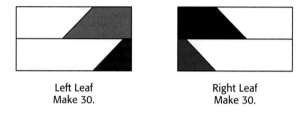

Left Leaf
Make 30.

Right Leaf
Make 30.

10. Sew the right and left leaf units to each side of the center leaf unit. Be careful not to catch the stem in the seam. Press.

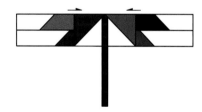

~~~~~~~~~~~~~~~~~~~~~~~~~~~~~~~

Remarks from Retta

Baste the stem in place, if desired, to keep it out of the way.

~~~~~~~~~~~~~~~~~~~~~~~~~~~~~~~

11. Center the 7½" light print triangle on the bottom of the leaf unit; sew together. Press toward the large triangle.

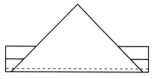

12. Sew the leaf unit to the Flower unit, having right sides together and matching the centers of the flower and leaves.

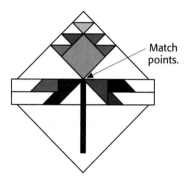

Match points.

13. Trim and square the block to 8" x 8", measuring ¼" from the leaf points.

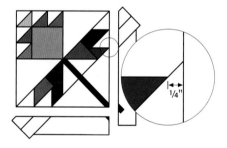

¼"

14. Hand stitch the stem in place, leaving the lower 1" unstitched.

15. Measure 1" up from the bottom point of the block and draw a line across the block at a 45° angle to the sides. Position the 2¼" brown triangle on the line, with the points extending ⅜" on each side. Stitch ¼" from the line. Press toward the edge of the block; trim the stem even with the seam allowance to eliminate bulk. Trim the edges even with the block and baste the raw edges in place.

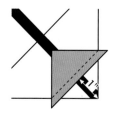

Assembly and Finishing

As you assemble the quilt, you may find it necessary to change some pressing directions for ease in matching points.

1. Make half-square-triangles for the center of the quilt and the inner rows using the 4⅝" dark, medium, and light squares. Pair the squares together in the following combinations: 4 each of dark with medium; 18 each of medium with light; 6 each of light with light; and 4 each of light with background. Using a pencil and a ruler, draw a diagonal line from corner to corner on the wrong side of the lighter squares. Stitch ¼" from each side of the marked lines. Cut on the marked lines. Press half of the seams toward the darker fabric and the other half toward the lighter fabric. These are the blocks for the inner part of the quilt and borders.

2. Using the illustration as a guide, assemble six rows using 29 of the Flower blocks, the 29 light print 8" x 4¼" rectangles, six half-square-triangle blocks, six 4¼" square light blocks, and six 4¼" square medium-dark blocks. Press toward the rectangles. Sew the rows together.

3. Make half-square triangles for the outer rows using the 4⅝" squares as you did in step 2. Pair the squares in the following combinations: 25 each of dark with medium; 13 each of dark (include green) with dark fabrics. Press half of the seams toward the darker fabric and the other half toward the lighter fabric.

4. Referring to the color photo on page 42 and the illustration below, assemble the top border unit, inner bottom row, bottom border row, left side border unit, and right side border unit, including the remaining blocks and 4¼" squares. Note that there will be several extra 4¼" squares and two extra half-square triangles. This will give you some options for color placement.

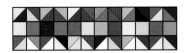

Top Border Unit

Inner Bottom Row

Bottom Border Row

Left Border Unit

Right Border Unit

5. Sew the inner bottom row to the bottom of the quilt. Press.

6. Add the top and bottom border units and then the side borders to the quilt.

7. Piece and trim the backing fabric so it is approximately 6" larger than the quilt top.
8. Layer the quilt with the batting and backing; baste. Quilt as desired.
9. Refer to "Finishing" on page 77 for details if needed. Trim the batting and backing fabric so the edges are even with the quilt top. Bind the quilt and add a label.

Snow Crystal

Designed, pieced, and quilted by Retta Warehime.
This wall hanging will warm the new home of my friend Rozan Meacham.

Finished Quilt: 36" x 43½"

Finished Block: 6"

When life gets stressful, I sit down and sew. Piecing these 6" blocks helped me get through the busy holiday season. I took this traditional old block design and made it smaller and easier to construct. This quilt uses just three colors for a time-honored and very soothing quilt. I love the way the cornerstones in the sashing create the diagonal movement in the quilt and add to the look of snow crystals. Hang this quilt near a display of antique glassware, or make it in scrappy country colors to complement any collection you have.

Materials

Yardages are based on 42"-wide fabrics.

1½ yards of light print for background

1¼ yards of red print for blocks and border

⅝ yard of black print for accent border and binding

1⅝ yards of fabric for backing

42" x 50" piece of batting

Cutting

From light print, cut:

4 strips, 1½" x 42"

6 strips, 1½" x 42"; cut into 144 squares, 1½" x 1½"

2 strips, 2½" x 42"; cut into 48 rectangles, 1½" x 2½"

4 strips, 2½" x 42"

2 strips, 6½" x 42"; cut into 31 rectangles, 2" x 6½"

From red print, cut:

4 strips, 1½" x 42"

4 strips, 1½" x 42"; cut into 96 squares, 1½" x 1½"

1 strip, 2" x 42"; cut into 20 squares, 2" x 2"

3 strips, 2½" x 42"; cut into 48 rectangles,
    2½" x 1½", and 12 squares, 2½" x 2½"

4 strips, 3¾" x 42"

From black print, cut:

3 strips, 1¼" x 42"

4 strips, 2½" x 42"

Block Assembly

1. Sew two 1½" x 42" red print and light print strips together to make four strip sets as shown. Cut the strip sets into 96 segments, 1½" wide.

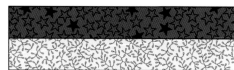

Make 4 strip sets.
Cut 96 segments.

2. Sew two segments from step 1 together to make a Four Patch block. Repeat to make 48.

Make 48.

3. Using a pencil and ruler, draw a diagonal line from corner to corner on the wrong side of all the 1½" red squares. Position each red square on top of a 2½" x 1½" light print rectangle, right sides together, matching left edges. Stitch on the drawn line. Trim the seam to ¼"; press toward the red. Repeat for the other side. Repeat to make a total of 48 of unit A.

Unit A
Make 48.

4. Using the same method as in step 3, sew a 1½" light print square to each side of a 2½" x 1½" red rectangle. Press toward the light print. Repeat to make a total of 48 of unit B.

Unit B
Make 48.

5. Sew units A and B together as shown. Make 48.

Make 48.

6. Position 1½" light print squares on opposite corners of a 2½" red print square, right sides together. Stitch on the drawn line. Trim seam to ¼"; press toward the light print. Repeat for the opposite corners. Make a total of 12 of unit C.

Unit C
Make 12.

7. Arrange the units from steps 5 and 6 with the Four Patch blocks, as shown. Sew the units together in rows; press. Join the rows and repeat to make 12 blocks.

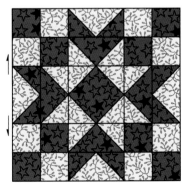

Make 12.

8. Make five sashing rows using the 2" red print squares and the 2" x 6½" light print background rectangles.

Make 5.

9. Assemble four rows of three blocks each, and four 2" x 6½" light print sashing rectangles in each row. Press toward the light print sashing.

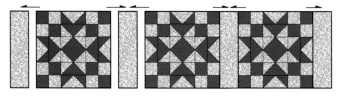

Make 4.

10. Join the four rows of blocks with the sashing rows. Press seams toward the sashing.

11. Referring to "Borders" on page 74, measure and trim the 1¼" black print inner border strips and sew them to the sides of the quilt top first, and then to the top and bottom. Repeat for the 2½"-wide light print borders and 3¾"-wide red outer borders.

12. Piece and trim the backing fabric so it is approximately 6" larger than the quilt top.

13. Layer the quilt top with the batting and backing; baste. Quilt as desired.

14. Refer to "Finishing" on page 77 for details if needed. Trim the batting and backing so they are even with the quilt top. Bind the quilt and add a label.

Star Steps

Finished Quilt: 36" x 36"
Finished Blocks: 6"

These Star blocks seem to dance around the center stars and diamonds. I chose reproduction Civil War fabrics for these blocks, and the design really allows the fabrics to shine and take center stage. Decorating options are almost unlimited with the versatile size of this quilt. Hang it on a wall above a piece of antique furniture or near a grouping of your favorite collectibles. Drape it over a cupboard door, or use it on an antique table with the stars tumbling off the sides.

Materials

Yardages are based on 42"-wide fabrics unless otherwise noted.

20 fat quarters or scraps for Star blocks

1½ yards of light print for background

⅜ yard of medium print for diamonds

1⅜ yard of fabric for backing

⅜ yard of fabric for binding

42" x 42" piece of batting

Cutting

From each fat quarter, cut:
8 squares, 2" x 2"
1 square, 3½" x 3½"

From light print, cut:
16 strips, 2" x 42"; cut into 80 squares, 2" x 2",
    80 rectangles, 2" x 3½", 12 rectangles, 2" x 6½",
    and 4 strips, 2" x 18½"
4 strips, 3½" x 42"; cut into 20 squares, 3½" x 3½",
    4 rectangles, 3½" x 6½", and 4 rectangles,
    3½" x 9½"

From medium print, cut:
5 squares, 6½" x 6½"

From binding fabric, cut:
4 strips, 2½" x 42"

Remarks from Retta
This is a wonderful project for showcasing a collection of fat quarters. You can feature your favorite prints in the centers of the stars and in the diamond blocks.

Designed, pieced, and quilted by Retta Warehime.
My friend Becky Hudon will receive this quilt; I chose the fabrics
specifically for the plum-colored wall where it will hang in her home.

Block Assembly

I made each of the Star blocks in my quilt different. Follow the steps below to make one Star block at a time. Mix and match the star center and points as desired. Make a total of 20 blocks.

1. Using a pencil and ruler, draw a diagonal line from corner to corner on the back of the 2" squares for the star points. Position a square on top of a 2" x 3½" light print rectangle as shown, with right sides together. Stitch on the drawn line. Trim the seam to ¼"; press seam toward the star fabric. Repeat for the right edge. Make 4 star-point units.

Make 4
for each block.

2. Sew one 2" background square to each end of two star-point units.

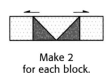

Make 2
for each block.

3. Sew one star-point unit to each side of a 3½" star-center square. Assemble the block in rows.

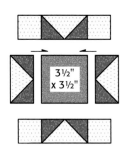 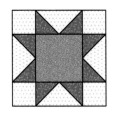

4. Repeat steps 1 through 3 to make 20 Star blocks.

5. Position two 3½" light print squares on opposite corners of a 6½" medium print square, right sides together. Draw a diagonal line, corner to corner as shown, and sew on the line. Trim the seam to ¼"; press toward the background. Repeat for the two remaining corners. Make 5.

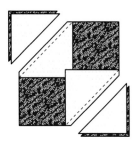 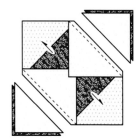

Make 5.

Assembly and Finishing

Lay out the Star blocks to arrange the colors before assembling.

1. Sew 3½" x 6½" light print rectangles to four Star blocks as shown. Then sew 3½" x 9½" rectangles to the side. Make two each of units A and B.

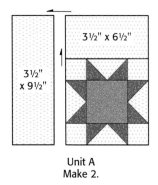 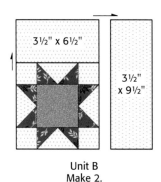

Unit A
Make 2.

Unit B
Make 2.

2. Sew 2" x 6½" light print rectangles to the sides of three Star blocks as shown. Sew the star blocks together in a vertical row and sew a 2" x 18½" light print strip to the side. Repeat to make four of unit C.

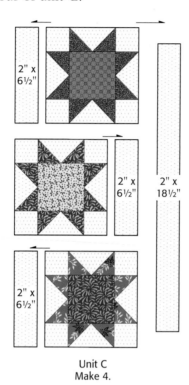

Unit C
Make 4.

3. Arrange the remaining four Star blocks and the five diamond blocks in rows as shown for the center section. Sew the blocks together and press toward the diamond blocks. Sew the rows together. Press away from center.

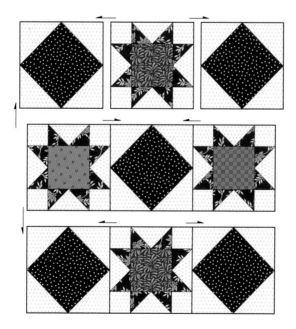

4. Sew a unit A to the left side of unit C and a unit B to the right side. Make two.

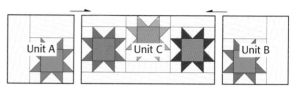

Make 2.

5. Sew one unit C to each side of the center section.

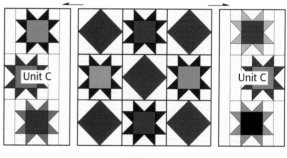

Make 1.

6. Sew an A–B–C unit to the top and bottom of the center section. Press.

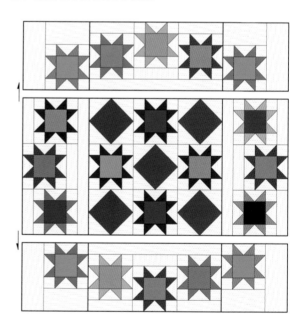

7. Piece and trim the backing fabric so it is approximately 6" larger than the quilt top.
8. Layer the quilt top with the batting and backing; baste. Quilt as desired.
9. Refer to "Finishing" on page 77 for details if needed. Trim the batting and backing so the edges are even with the quilt top. Bind the quilt and add a label.

Carolyn Ann's Presents

Designed and pieced by Retta Warehime, quilted by Pam Clarke.
This quilt was designed and named for a young friend who was very special to our family.
It will be given to Ann Rettig, in memory of her daughter Carolyn Ann.

Finished Quilt: 63¾" x 73¾"

Finished Block: 16¼" x 13¾"

Here's a chance to combine several of your favorite colors together in a quilt. My favorites are the dark shades of green and red. I included the gold to add a sparkle throughout. Curl up on the sofa with this quilt, and display it on an antique quilt rack when you're not using it. You'll want to keep it handy and out in full view to enjoy the wonderful mosaic of colors and the pattern of diagonal movement.

Materials

Yardages are based on 42"-wide fabrics.

2⅝ yards of light print for background

⅞ yard *each* of three green prints

¾ yard *each* of three red prints

1¼ yards of gold print

4 yards of fabric for backing

¾ yard of fabric for binding

70" x 80" piece of batting

Cutting

From *each* of the 3 reds, cut:
11 strips, 1¾" x 42"
6 squares, 1¾" x 1¾"

From *each* of the 3 greens, cut:
14 strips, 1¾" x 42"
6 squares, 1¾" x 1¾"

From gold, cut:
21 strips, 1¾" x 42"
6 squares, 1¾" x 1¾"

From light print, cut:
48 strips, 1¾" x 42"
15 squares, 1¾" x 1¾"

From the binding fabric, cut:
8 strips, 2½" x 42"

Piecing the Blocks

1. The blocks are made from 1¾" segments cut from five different strip sets made up of red, green, and gold strips. Assemble strip sets A through E, referring to the diagrams for color placement and the number of each strip set to make. You can randomly place the red, green, and gold strips, but position the background strips specifically where shown. Note that strip set A has 6 strips and all the others have just 5 strips. Press all the seam allowances in the direction of the arrows on the diagrams.

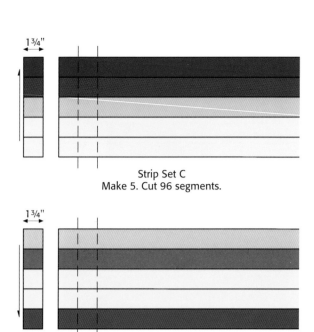

Strip Set C
Make 5. Cut 96 segments.

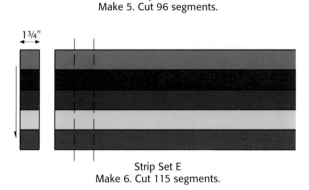

Strip Set D
Make 5. Cut 96 segments.

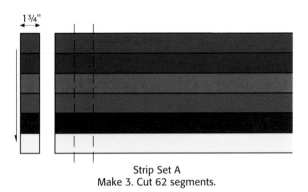

Strip Set A
Make 3. Cut 62 segments.

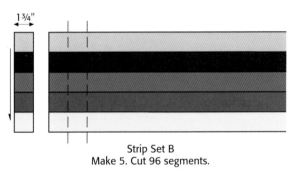

Strip Set B
Make 5. Cut 96 segments.

Strip Set E
Make 6. Cut 115 segments.

2. Cut the strip sets into 1¾" segments as indicated in the diagrams above.
3. Set aside 24 segments cut from strip set E. Sew the remaining 91 segments from strip set E together end to end to make one long E strip.

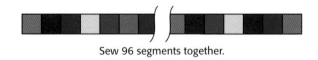

Sew 96 segments together.

4. Referring to the diagram, assemble 24 each of unit 1 and unit 2. Note that both units use the same segments, but they are arranged as mirror images of one another.

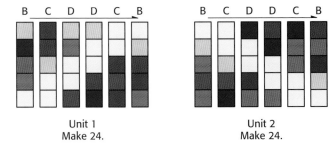

Unit 1
Make 24.

Unit 2
Make 24.

5. Join a unit 1 and unit 2 with a strip set E segment in between. Press the seam allowances toward the E segment. Repeat to make 24 of these half blocks.

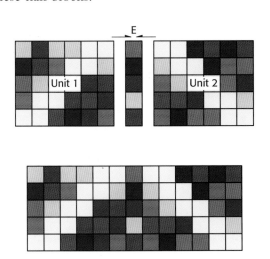

Make 24 half blocks.

6. Sew two segments cut from strip set A to either side of a 1¾" background fabric square. Note that the background square ends of the A segments are sewn to the center background square. Repeat to make 15 of these sashing 1 strips.

Sashing 1
Make 15.

7. Sew two segments cut from strip set A to either side of a 1¾" red, green, or gold square. For these units, the background squares on the A segments are on the outer edges of the strip. Repeat to make 12 of these sashing 2 strips.

Sashing 2
Make 12.

8. To make sashing 3 strips, use your seam ripper to remove four 11-square segments from the long E strip made in step 3. Sew together three 1¾" red, green, or gold squares, four strip set A segments, and two of the 11-square E strips, as shown below. Repeat to make two sashing 3 strips.

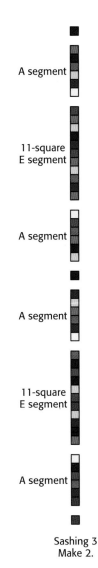

A segment

11-square
E segment

A segment

A segment

11-square
E segment

A segment

Sashing 3
Make 2.

9. Sew two half blocks from step 5 to either side of a sashing 2 strip from step 6 to assemble a block. Repeat to make 12 blocks.

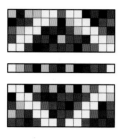

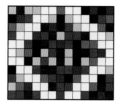

Make 12.

Assembling the Quilt

1. Make a vertical panel using five sashing 1 strips and four blocks in each section as shown. Repeat to make a total of three panels.

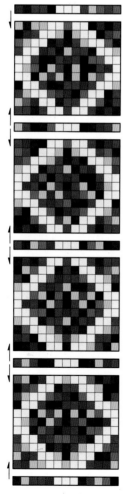

Make 3 panels.

2. Join the vertical panels and two sashing 3 strips. Press away from the sashing strips.

Sashing 3 strips

Adding the Borders

This quilt has a series of five borders. Borders 1, 3, and 5 are made of 1¾" background fabric strips; borders 2 and 4 are made of the long strip of E segments that were joined together in step 3 of "Piecing the Blocks" on page 62.

1. Sew the remaining 1¾"-wide background fabric strips together, end to end. Trim the long strip to the following lengths:

   2 strips, 61¾" long, for side border 1

   2 strips, 54¼" long, for top and bottom border 1

   2 strips, 66¾" long, for side border 3

   2 strips, 59¼" long, for top and bottom border 3

   2 strips, 71¾" long, for side border 5

   2 strips, 64¼" long, for top and bottom border 5

2. From the long, E strip, cut off:

   2 segments of 51 squares for side border 2

   2 segments of 45 squares for top and bottom border 2

   2 segments of 55 squares for side border 4

   2 segments of 49 squares for top and bottom border 4

3. Sew the borders to the quilt, always adding the sides first, and then the top and bottom of each border. Press the seams toward the background fabric borders.

Finishing the Quilt

1. Trim the quilt backing so it is approximately 6" larger than the quilt top. Layer the quilt top, batting, and backing, and baste.

2. Hand or machine quilt as desired. The quilt shown is machine quilted with green and beige variegated thread in an allover holly leaf and berry pattern that nicely complements the busy patchwork pattern.

3. Refer to "Finishing" on page 77 for details if needed. Trim the batting and backing fabric even with the quilt. Bind the quilt and add a label.

Quiltmaking Essentials

The purpose of this book is to provide quilters with beautiful quilt projects using quick and accurate techniques. On the pages that follow you will find all the information needed for the successful completion of your quilts. Refer to it as needed during the construction of your quilts. It is designed for beginners and novice quilters, but you never know when you'll learn something new or be inspired to try a new way of doing something.

Fabrics

I always use 100%-cotton fabrics. Cotton is very durable and holds a crease after pressing. It softens after each washing and is preferred by most quiltmakers. A good guideline in selecting fabrics for a quilting project is to buy the best you can afford (although the most expensive fabric is not necessarily the best). Look for tightly woven fabric with a soft feel and drape. If you are going to invest your time in a project, you want the materials to be of good quality so that it will last for a very long time.

Sufficient yardage requirements are provided in the materials lists for all the projects in this book. They are based on 42"-wide fabrics that provide at least 40" of usable fabric after pre-washing and after selvages have been trimmed away. To vary the look of any design, use an assortment of scraps and purchase only those fabrics you need to complete the project you have chosen. Several of the quilts in this book were made from the fabrics in my stash; all I bought were new background fabrics.

I suggest prewashing all fabrics to preshrink them and test for colorfastness. This step removes any excess dye and any chemicals added in the finishing. Iron the fabric before cutting to insure accuracy. You can use spray sizing to add back the body lost in the wash.

The Antique Look

If you want your quilt to have that crinkled, vintage look, do not prewash the fabrics before cutting or sewing. Piece the top, layer it with an unwashed 100%-cotton batting, and quilt it by hand or machine. When the quilt is finished, machine wash and dry it so that the fabrics and batting shrink as a unit. This will give your quilt an old-fashioned, antique look almost instantly.

Supplies

Sewing machine: For machine piecing, you'll need a sewing machine that is in good working condition. If a ¼" foot is available for your machine, I recommend that you purchase one. It is worth its weight in gold! A walking foot or darning foot makes machine quilting much easier.

Marking tools: A variety of tools are available to mark fabric when tracing around templates or marking quilting designs. Always test your marker on a scrap of fabric to make sure you can remove the marks easily.

Needles: Always use a new needle when you start a new project. For machine piecing, a size 10/70 or 12/80 works best. For machine quilting, use a 12/80 or 14/90. For hand appliqué, choose a needle that will glide easily through the edges of the appliqué pieces. Size 10 (fine) to size 12 (very fine) Sharp needles are good choices.

Pins: My favorite pins are long with yellow heads. Try different sizes; your preference may be different. Many quilters prefer silk pins for pinning patchwork pieces. Smaller, ½" to ¾" sequin pins work best for appliqué.

Rotary-cutting tools: You will need a rotary cutter, cutting mat, and clear acrylic ruler. Rotary-cutting rulers are available in a variety of sizes, the most essential sizes being: 6" x 24", 12" x 12", 6" x 6", and my favorite, 6" x 12".

Scissors: Reserve your best scissors for cutting fabric only. Use craft scissors to cut paper, fusible web, and template plastic. Small, sharp scissors or thread snips are handy for cutting threads.

Seam ripper: I keep one handy whenever I sit down to sew. The sharper the seam ripper the better—it will allow you to get back to sewing as soon as possible. I cut every fourth or fifth stitch, and then pull the one long thread from the other side.

Template plastic: Use clear or frosted plastic (available at quilt shops) to make durable, accurate templates.

Thread: Use a good-quality, all-purpose cotton thread. Use the same thread in the bobbin, as the stitching is always more even if the bobbin is wound from the same thread that is used on top. I use cream, white, and gray thread most often for piecing.

Rotary Cutting

I love the speed and accuracy of this fabric cutting method. I rely on quick-and-easy rotary cutting to help me cut and piece quilts on a deadline! All cutting measurements include standard ¼"-wide seam allowances. If you are unfamiliar with rotary cutting, read the brief introduction that starts below. For more detailed information, see the book *Shortcuts: A Concise Guide to Rotary Cutting* by Donna Lynn Thomas (Martingale & Company, 1999).

1. Fold the fabric in half, matching selvages. Align the crosswise and lengthwise grains as much as possible. Place the folded edge closest to you on the cutting mat. Align a square ruler along the folded edge of the fabric. Place a long, straight ruler to the left of the square ruler, just covering the uneven raw edges on the left side of the fabric. Remove the square ruler and cut along the right edge of the long ruler, rolling the rotary cutter away from you. Discard this strip. (Reverse this procedure if you are left-handed.)

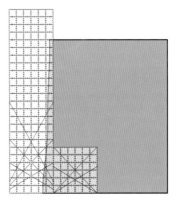

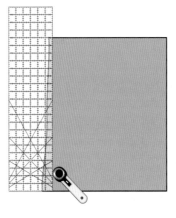

2. To cut strips, align the newly cut edge of the fabric with the ruler markings at the required width. For example, to cut a 3"-wide strip, place the 3" ruler mark on the edge of the fabric.

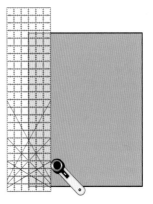

3. To cut squares, cut a strip of the required width and trim the selvage ends off. Align the left edge of the strip with the correct ruler markings, the same measurement as the width of the strips. Cut the strip into squares until you have the number needed.

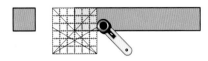

4. To cut half-square triangles, begin by cutting a square ⅞" larger than the finished size of the short side of the triangle. Then cut the square once diagonally, from corner to corner. Each square yields two half-square triangles. The short sides of each triangle are on the straight grain of the fabric.

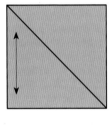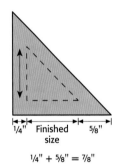

¼" Finished ⅝"
size

¼" + ⅝" = ⅞"

5. To cut a quarter-square triangle, begin by cutting a square 1¼" larger than the finished size of the long side of the triangle. Then cut the square twice diagonally, from corner to corner. Each square yields four quarter-square triangles. The long side of each triangle is on the straight grain of the fabric.

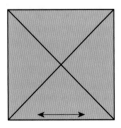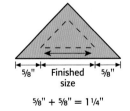

⅝" Finished ⅝"
size

⅝" + ⅝" = 1¼"

Machine Piecing

All of the quilts in this book were designed for the quickest piecing possible. But, do take the time to establish an exact ¼" seam allowance on your machine before beginning to sew. Some machines have a special quilting foot that measures exactly ¼" from the center needle position to the edge of the foot. This feature allows you to use the edge of the presser foot to guide the fabric for a perfect ¼"-wide seam allowance. If your machine doesn't have such a foot, you may be able to purchase a generic ¼" foot for it. Or, you can create a seam guide by placing a piece of masking tape ¼" away from the needle on the bed of your sewing machine. By determining an exact ¼"-wide seam allowance for your piecing, your results will be more accurate, and your quilts will go together successfully.

Once you have determined an exact ¼" seam allowance, set your machine to sew 12 to 15 stitches per inch for normal piecing. I suggest that you measure your blocks once they are pieced. They should measure ½" larger than the finished size given with each project. Checking the block measurement will help ensure that any sashings and borders will fit exactly.

To make for the easiest matching of seam intersections and points, always work with opposing seam allowances whenever possible. When seam allowances are pressed in opposite directions, the seams will "lock" into position and line up exactly. Make sure the seam allowance on the bottom is pressed so that it moves easily over the feed dogs. Keep the top seam allowance pressed in the opposite direction. Sometimes I find it necessary to change the pressing direction as the block is assembled to achieve opposing seams. See also "Pressing" on page 69.

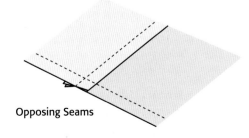

Opposing Seams

CHAIN PIECING

Chain piecing saves time and thread and is especially useful when making many identical or similar units. You can use it when making most of the quilt blocks in this book.

1. Stack patches right sides together (pin if you like). Sew the first pair of pieces from cut edge to cut edge. Stop sewing at the end of the seam, but do not backstitch or clip the thread.
2. Feed the next pair of pieces under the presser foot, as close as possible to the first pair. Sew the seam, and continue feeding pieces through the machine without cutting the threads in between.
3. When all the pairs are sewn, remove the chain from the machine. It will resemble a line of laundry. Clip the threads, and place the units on your pressing surface.

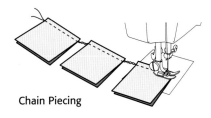

Chain Piecing

Pressing

The traditional rule in quilt making is to press seams to one side, toward the darker color wherever possible. First, press the seams in the desired direction from the wrong side of the fabric (I call this a tack press); then press the seams from the right side. Press carefully to avoid distorting the shapes. Remember, there are always exceptions to the rule and it may be necessary to re-press as you assemble your block or rows.

Appliqué Basics

I have included instructions here for hand, freezer-paper, and fusible appliqué. Feel free to use your favorite method regardless of the method described in the project. Just be sure to adapt the pattern pieces and project instructions as necessary.

MAKING TEMPLATES

You will need to make a template of the appliqué pattern. I prefer to make templates from clear plastic, because it is durable and you can see through it when tracing or trying to fussy cut.

1. Place template plastic over each pattern piece and trace with a fine-line permanent marker. Do not add seam allowances.
2. Cut out the templates on the drawn line. You need one template for each different motif or shape.
3. Write the pattern name and grain-line arrow (if applicable) on the template.

HAND APPLIQUÉ

In traditional hand appliqué, the seam allowances are turned under before the appliqué is stitched to the background fabric. Two traditional methods for turning under the edges are needle-turn appliqué and freezer-paper appliqué. You can use either method to turn under the raw edges, and then use the hand-appliqué stitch or blind stitch to attach the shapes to your background fabric.

Freezer-Paper Appliqué

Freezer paper is coated on one side and is often used by quilters for appliqué and other purposes. I use it as a guide to turn under seam allowances before stitching; it also stabilizes the appliqué pieces during the stitching process to help make nearly perfect appliqué shapes.

1. Trace around the plastic template on the dull side (not the shiny side) of the freezer paper with a sharp pencil. You can also place the freezer paper, shiny side down, directly on top of the pattern and trace.

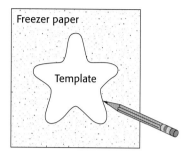

2. Cut out the traced design on the pencil line. Do not add seam allowances.
3. Place the freezer-paper templates, shiny side down, on the wrong side of the appliqué fabric. Iron the freezer-paper shape in place with a hot, dry iron. Leave at least ¾" between pieces.

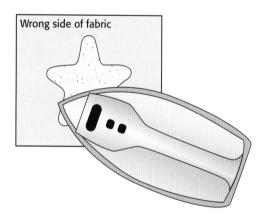

4. Cut around the fabric shape, adding ¼" seam allowances around all the edges.

5. Turn the seam allowance over the freezer-paper edges and baste by hand. Clip inner points and fold under the outer points. Trim excess fabric at outer points to reduce bulk if desired.

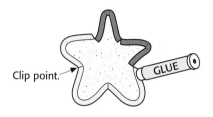

6. Pin or baste the design to the background fabric. Appliqué the design to the background with a small stitch and matching thread. Letting the needle travel under the background fabric, parallel to the edge of the appliqué, bring it up about ⅛" away, along the pattern line. As you bring the needle up, pierce the edge of the appliqué piece, catching only a few threads of the folded edge. Refer to "Traditional Appliqué Stitch" below for additional details.
7. Remove any basting stitches. Cut a slit in the background fabric behind the appliqué and remove the freezer paper with tweezers.

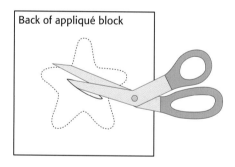

Traditional Appliqué Stitch

The traditional appliqué stitch or blind stitch is appropriate for sewing all appliqué shapes, including sharp points and curves.

1. Thread a needle with a single strand of thread approximately 18" long. Use a good quality cotton or silk thread in a color that closely matches the color of your appliqué. Knot the end.
2. Hide the knot by slipping the needle into the seam allowance from the wrong side of the appliqué piece, bringing it out on the fold line.

3. Work from right to left if you are right-handed, or from left to right if you are left-handed. To make the first stitch, insert the needle into the background right next to where the needle came out of the appliqué fabric. Bring the needle up through the edge of the appliqué, about ⅛" away from the first stitch. As you bring the needle up, pierce the basted or turned-under edge of the appliqué piece, catching only a few threads.

4. Repeat, to take a second stitch into the background block right next to where the thread came up through the appliqué. Bring the needle up about ⅛" away from the previous stitch, again catching the folded edge of the appliqué.

5. Pull the thread gently to secure the stitches, and continue.

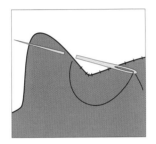

6. To end your stitching, pull the needle through to the wrong side. Behind the appliqué, take two small stitches, making knots by taking your needle through the loops. Clip the thread.

Remarks from Retta

To make certain that no thread tails show through the background fabric on the right side, take one more small stitch on the backside before clipping the thread to bring the needle out behind the appliqué piece. The tail of the thread will be hidden behind the appliqué fabric.

FUSIBLE APPLIQUÉ

Using fusible web is a fast and easy way to appliqué. I used this method to apply the stars in "Greggory's Quilt" on page 31. Use the pattern exactly as it appears, without adding a seam allowance. Always use lightweight fusible web if you will be stitching the edges by machine or by hand.

Refer to the manufacturer's directions when applying fusible web to your fabrics; each brand is a little different and pressing it too long may result in fusible web that doesn't stick well, although there is a product that you can sprinkle on the back to get your fusible web to fuse again. Look for it at your favorite quilt shop.

1. Trace or draw your shape on the paper side of the fusible web. Cut out the shape, leaving at least a ¼" margin all around.

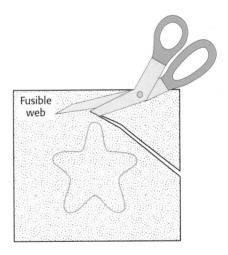

Fusible web

2. Fuse the shapes to the wrong side of your chosen appliqué fabric.

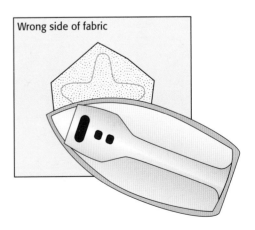

Wrong side of fabric

3. Cut out the shape exactly on the drawn line.

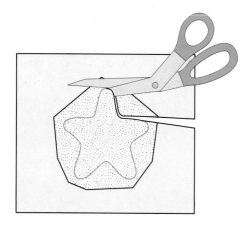

4. Remove the paper backing from the appliqué, position it on the background fabric, and fuse it in place with your iron.

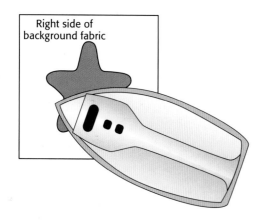

Right side of background fabric

5. Add decorative stitches by hand or machine around the edges of the fused appliqués, if desired. This adds a decorative touch, gives more depth to the appliqués, and ensures that the edges will be secure. Commonly used stitches include satin stitch and blanket stitch. The stars in "Greggory's Quilt" (page 31) were edged with a hand blanket stitch.

Close-Up View of Blanket Stitch

SQUARING UP BLOCKS

After stitching your quilt blocks, take the time to press them carefully. Then measure them and square them up. Make sure the size is ½" larger than the finished size. If your blocks vary slightly in size, trim the larger blocks to match the size of the smallest block. Be sure to trim all four sides; otherwise, your block will be lopsided. If your blocks are not the correct finished size, other components of the quilt will need to be adjusted. You may also need to adjust your seam allowances when joining the blocks together.

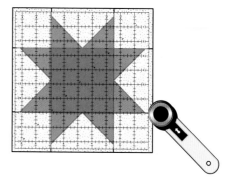

Remarks from Retta

Square up pieced units such as half-square-triangle units the same way as you would square up a block.

STRAIGHT SETTINGS

1. Arrange the blocks as shown in the diagram provided with each quilt.
2. Sew blocks together in horizontal or vertical rows, according to the quilt instructions. Press the seams in opposite directions from row to row (unless otherwise directed).

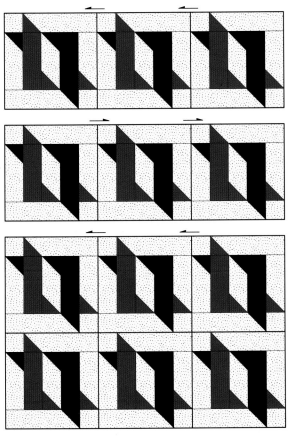

Straight-Set Quilt

3. Pin the rows together, being careful to match the block intersections from row to row. Sew the rows together and press the seams all in one direction.

DIAGONAL SETTINGS

1. Arrange the blocks, setting triangles, and corner triangles as shown in the diagram provided with the quilt instructions. The setting triangles and corner triangles will be larger than necessary and will be trimmed ¼" away from the corner points of the blocks when the quilt top is completed.
2. Sew the blocks and side setting triangles together in diagonal rows; press the seams in opposite directions from row to row (unless directed otherwise).
3. Sew the rows together, matching seams. Sew corner triangles on last.

Diagonally Set Quilt

Borders

For best results, always measure your quilt through the center before cutting or adding border strips. Quilts often tend to "grow" on the outer edges as they get larger, but remain the same through the center. Measure the quilt top through the center in both directions to determine how long to cut the border strips. This step ensures that your finished quilt will be as "square" as possible.

All of the quilts in this book call for plain border strips. The strips are cut along the crosswise grain and pieced together where extra length is needed. Always ease the quilt top to fit the border strips.

1. Measure the length of the quilt top through the center. From the crosswise grain, cut two border strips to that measurement, piecing as necessary. Mark the centers of the quilt edges and border strips. Pin the side borders to opposite sides of the quilt top, matching centers and ends and easing as necessary. Sew the border strips to the quilt top; press the seam allowances toward the borders.

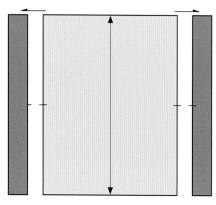

Measure center of quilt,
top to bottom. Mark centers.

2. Measure the width of the quilt top through the center, including the side borders just added. From the crosswise grain, cut two border strips to that measurement, piecing as necessary. Mark the centers of the quilt edges and the border strips. Pin the borders to the top and bottom edges of the quilt top, matching the center marks and ends and easing as necessary. Sew the border strips in place. Press the seams toward the border strips.

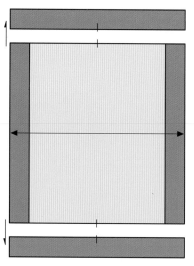

Measure center of quilt, side to
side, including border strips.
Mark centers.

Preparing to Quilt

Follow the directions in this section for layering, basting, and quilting if you plan to quilt by hand or on your home sewing machine. If you plan to have a professional machine quilter quilt your project, check with the quilter before preparing your finished quilt top in any way. Most of the quilts in this book were quilted using a long-arm quilting machine. To find a professional machine quilter in your area, check with your local quilt shop for referrals.

MARKING QUILTING DESIGNS

After you complete the quilt top, give it a final pressing. Make sure that the seams all lie flat and are going in the correct direction. For quilting in the ditch (along the seam lines) or for free-motion random designs, marking is not necessary. Masking tape can be used on a basted quilt to mark straight lines. Tape only small sections at a time and remove the tape when you stop quilting. If left on, sticky residue may be difficult to remove. If you plan to use detailed quilting patterns or complex designs, mark the quilt top before you baste the quilt layers together. Choose a marking tool that will be visible on your fabric and test it on scrap fabrics to be sure that the marks can be removed easily.

LAYERING AND BASTING THE QUILT

Cut the backing fabric and batting at least 4" to 6" larger than the quilt top. For large quilts, it is usually necessary to sew two or three lengths of fabric together to make a backing that is large enough. Always trim away the selvages before piecing the lengths together. Press the seams open to make quilting easier by minimizing bulk.

Two lengths of fabric with a center seam

1 fabric width

Partial fabric width

Batting comes packaged in standard bed sizes, or it can be purchased by the yard in many different weights or thicknesses. A thinner batting is best if you intend to quilt by hand or machine, and the quilt will have a nicer drape. I use a little heavier batting for wall hangings.

1. Spread the backing wrong side up on a flat, clean surface. Anchor it with pins, binder clips, or masking tape. Be careful not to stretch the backing out of shape.
2. Spread the batting over the backing, smoothing wrinkles from the center out.
3. Center the pressed quilt top on top of the batting. Again, smooth wrinkles from the center out, making sure the quilt-top edges are parallel to the edges of the backing.
4. Starting in the center, baste with needle and thread and work diagonally to each corner. Then baste a grid of horizontal and vertical lines 6" to 8" apart.

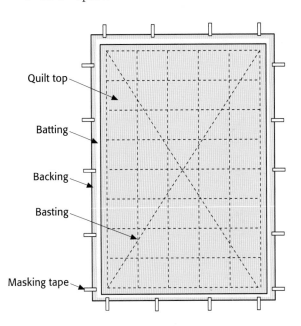

Note: For machine quilting, you may baste the layers with #2 rustproof safety pins. Place pins about 6" to 8" apart and remove safety pins as you go.

Machine Quilting

Machine quilting is suitable for all types of quilts. With machine quilting, you can quickly complete quilts and move on to the next project.

Marking the quilting design is optional. You will only need to mark your quilt if you select a complex design or plan to follow a grid. In most cases, quilts lend themselves to stitching in the ditch, outline quilting, or free-motion quilting in a random pattern.

For straight-line quilting (such as in the ditch), it is extremely helpful to have a walking foot to help feed the quilt layers through the machine without shifting or puckering. Some machines have a built-in walking foot; most machines require a separate attachment.

Walking Foot

For free-motion quilting, you need a darning foot and the ability to drop or cover the feed dogs on your machine. Consult your sewing-machine instruction manual if you need help. With free-motion quilting, you guide the fabric in the direction of the design rather than turning the entire quilt under the needle. With a little practice you can quickly become quite proficient.

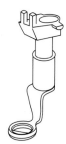

Darning Foot

Hand Quilting

Hand quilting is the time-honored method of holding the layers of a quilt together, but it does take longer than machine quilting. To quilt by hand, use a short, sturdy needle called a Between. Start with a size 8 and gradually work toward using smaller needles (the higher the number, the smaller the needle). You will also need a thimble for your middle finger, quilting thread, and a hoop or frame to hold the quilt sandwich for stitching.

1. Thread your needle with a length of quilting thread about 18" long. Make a small knot in one end. Insert the needle into the top layer and batting of the quilt about ½" from where you want to begin stitching. Pull the needle out at the point where stitching will begin and gently pull the thread until the knot pops through the fabric and into the batting.

2. Using your thimble to control the needle, insert the needle vertically into the quilt. Place your other hand underneath the quilt so you can feel the needle point with the tip of your finger when the needle is through the layers. Rock the needle back up through the layers and down again until you have three or four stitches on the needle. Pull the needle through and repeat the stitching process.

3. To end a line of quilting, make a small knot close to the last stitch; then make a backstitch and slide the needle through the batting about ½" away. Bring the needle up and gently pull on the thread until the knot pops into the batting. Snip the thread at the quilt's surface.

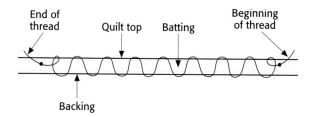

Finishing

Congratulations! You're close to having a finished quilt! Follow the steps below for adding an optional hanging sleeve, binding, and a label.

HANGING SLEEVE

If your quilt will be hung on a wall, you may want to add a permanent hanging sleeve. A hanging sleeve creates a secure space to insert a rod and will support the quilt evenly. If your quilt has a hanging sleeve, it is quite simple to change the look of a room; simply slip the quilt off the rod, replace it with another quilt from your collection, and place the rod back on the wall.

> ### Remarks from Retta
> Be sure to hang your quilts out of direct sunlight to prevent fading.

1. From the leftover quilt backing fabric or other coordinating fabric, cut a strip 6" to 8" wide and 1" shorter than the width of your quilt. Fold and press the ends under ½", then ½" again to make a hem. Stitch the hems.

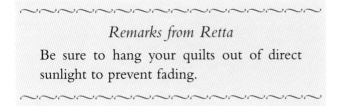

Fold ends under ½" twice.

2. Fold the fabric strip in half lengthwise, wrong sides together, and baste the raw edges to the top of the quilt back. The top edge of the sleeve will be secured when the binding is sewn on the quilt.

Baste sleeve to top edge of quilt.

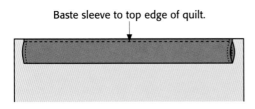

3. Finish the sleeve after the binding has been attached by blind-stitching the bottom of the sleeve in place. Before sewing the bottom edge in place, push the sleeve up just a bit to provide a little excess fabric for the hanging rod; this will keep the rod from putting strain on the quilt.

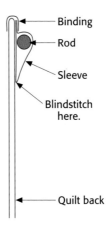

- Binding
- Rod
- Sleeve
- Blindstitch here.
- Quilt back

BINDING

I prefer French double-fold binding. For all the quilts in this book, I cut the bindings 2½" wide across the width of fabric and then pieced strips to obtain the desired length. You will need enough strips to go around the perimeter of the quilt, plus 10" for seams and finishing the corners.

First trim the batting and backing even with the quilt top. Use your longest ruler and a square ruler if you have one to make the quilt as square and straight as possible. Make and add a hanging sleeve, if desired, before adding the binding (see "Hanging Sleeve" at left). Use a walking foot, if you have one, when sewing the binding to the quilt. It helps to feed all the layers through the machine evenly.

Mitered Binding

1. Join the binding strips together to make one long strip. Sew the strips right sides together at right angles, stitching on the diagonal from corner to corner as shown. Trim the seam to ¼" and press open.

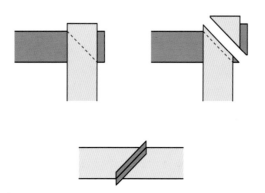

2. Fold the binding strip in half lengthwise, wrong sides together, and press. Turn under ¼" at a 45° angle at one end of the strip and press. Turning the end under at an angle distributes the bulk so that you will have a smoother connection where the two ends of the binding meet.

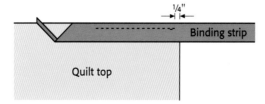

3. Begin on a side of the quilt and stitch the binding to the quilt, using a ¼" seam allowance and keeping the raw edges even with the quilt top edge. End the stitching ¼" from the corner of the quilt, and backstitch. Clip the thread.

4. Turn the quilt 90° so that you'll be stitching down the next side. Fold the binding up, away from the quilt. Then fold the binding back down onto itself, aligning the raw edges with the side

of the quilt top to be sewn next. Begin stitching ¼" from the corner, backstitching to secure the stitches. Repeat the process on the remaining sides and corners of the quilt.

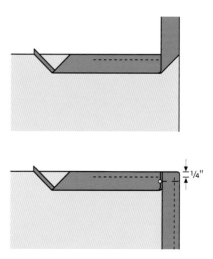

5. When you reach the starting point of the binding, stop stitching. Overlap the starting edge of binding by about 1", and cut away any excess binding, trimming the end at a 45° angle. Tuck the end of the binding into the fold and finish sewing the binding in place.

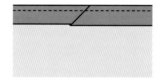

6. Fold the binding over the raw edges of the quilt to the back so that the finished edge just covers the row of machine stitching. Blindstitch the binding in place, forming a miter at each corner.

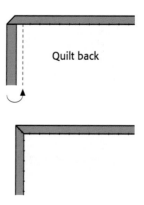

Lapped Binding

1. Follow step 1 of "Mitered Binding" on page 78. Fold the binding strip in half lengthwise, wrong sides together, and press. Measure the quilt top vertically through the center and cut two strips of binding to this length for side bindings. Use a ¼" seam allowance and stitch the binding to the sides of the quilt, keeping the raw edges of the binding even with the trimmed edges of quilt.

2. Fold the binding over the edges of the quilt to the back, with the folded edge covering the row of machine stitching. Blindstitch the binding in place.

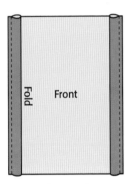 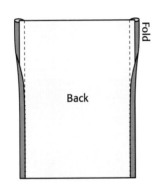

Match raw edges.

3. Measure the quilt top horizontally through the center and cut two strips of binding to this measurement, plus 1". Fold under ½" on each end of binding and press. Stitch the binding to the top and bottom of the quilt, keeping raw edges even with quilt-top edges. Fold the binding to the back and finish the same as the side bindings. Slipstitch the ends closed.

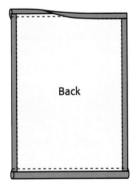

ADDING A LABEL

Please be sure to sign and date your quilts by adding a label to the back. Include the name of the quilt, your name, the quilter's name (if different from you), your city and state, the date, and the intended recipient, if desired. If you document your quilt with a simple label, future generations will be able to learn a little bit of its history.

Stabilize your label fabric by ironing a piece of freezer paper to the wrong side. Use a fine-tipped, permanent fabric pen to record the information on the fabric. Attach it to the back of the quilt with small stitches or blanket stitch it in place. You may also type, print, or embroider your information on the fabric before sewing it to the back of your quilt.

Star Steps
by
Retta Warehime
Kennewick, WA, 2003
36" x 36"
Made for Becky Hudon.

About the Author

Retta Warehime was introduced to quilting and designing quilts more than 20 years ago, thanks to her friends Jackie Wolff, Debbie Mumm, and Ann Weisbeck.

She has lived in Kennewick, Washington, for 15 years. Before that, she lived in Spokane. She keeps busy designing quilts, teaching, writing, and publishing books for her company Sew Cherished. She also designs quilts for Fiber Mosaics and is their editor in chief. Retta has four children and two grandchildren. In addition, she and her husband host two WHL hockey players who live in their home eight months out of the year.

Designing and quilting give Retta great pleasure, calming her nerves and soothing her soul. Her inspiration comes from living life to the fullest, and she is continually motivated by her desire to share the attributes of quilting with everyone. One of her greatest pleasures comes from giving quilts away and teaching others the joy of quilting.